Key West

Photo Journal

Craig & Cheri Howard

Cover Image: Smathers Beach

Acknowledgements: Thank you Bob

Copyright ©2001 Craig and Cheri Howard

Designed and Published: Fonts & Film
1103 Truman Avenue, Key West, FL
email: craighowardkeywest@yahoo.com

Printed in Hong Kong

ISBN: 0-9713531-0-7

East Martello Museum

Key West Lighthouse

Houseboat Row

Southernmost Point

Port of Key West

Roseate Spoonbill

Great Egret

White Ibis

Greene Street at Duval

Duval Street at Night

Wreckers Monument at Key West Sculpture Garden

IN MEMORY
OF THE VICTIMS
OF THE
DISASTER
OF
U.S. BATTLE-SHIP
"MAINE"
IN HAVANA HARBOR
FEB. 15, 1898.

ERECTED BY
CITIZENS
OF KEY WEST, FLA.

Key West Cemetery

Bocce Courts and Nature Trail at Indigenous Park

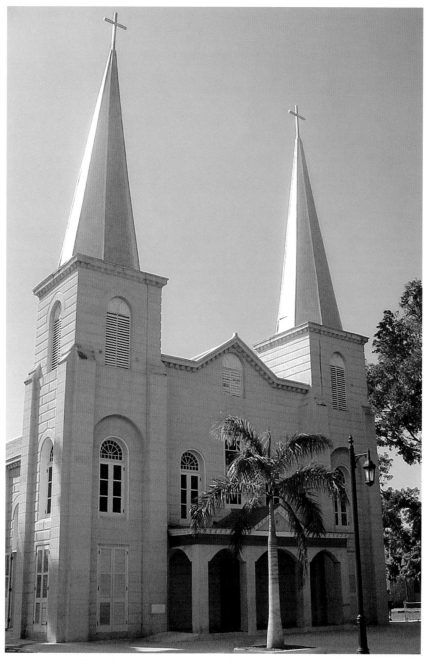

St. Mary Star of the Sea Catholic Church

St. Paul's Episcopal Church

Boardwalk and Salt Ponds at Little Hamaca Park

LaConcha Hotel

San Carlos Institute

AIDS Memorial

Old Stone Methodist Church

Key West Garden Club at West Martello

Giant Swallowtail

Wall Street

Audubon House

Cuban Banana

Hibiscus

Duval Street

Historic Seaport District

Front Street

Key West Seaport

First Union Bank Building

Custom House

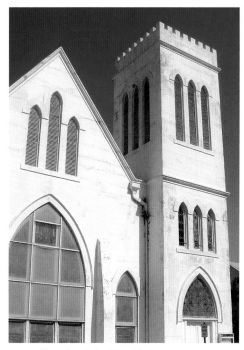

Church of God in Christ

Monroe County Court House

Fort Zachary Taylor State Park

Higgs Beach

Performer at Mallory Square's Sunset Celebration

Simonton Street Pier

José Marti Monument at Bay View Park

CORAL ISLE BAR
FREE BEER *tomorrow...*

DIVA's

KEY WEST WOMAN'S CLUB
ESTABLISHED 1915

Halfred MOTEL

BAR & GRILL
Pi's
LATE NIGHT

RED BARN THEATRE

HOG'S BREATH SALOON

KOZUCHI

HISTORIC SEAPORT
AT THE KEY WEST BIGHT

CONCH
CIGAR
FAC TORY
REPUBLIC

Southernmost House

Curry Mansion

Indigenous Park

Richard Peacon House (Octagon House)

Key West City Marina

Federal Court House

Old City Hall

Waterfront Playhouse

Lazy Way